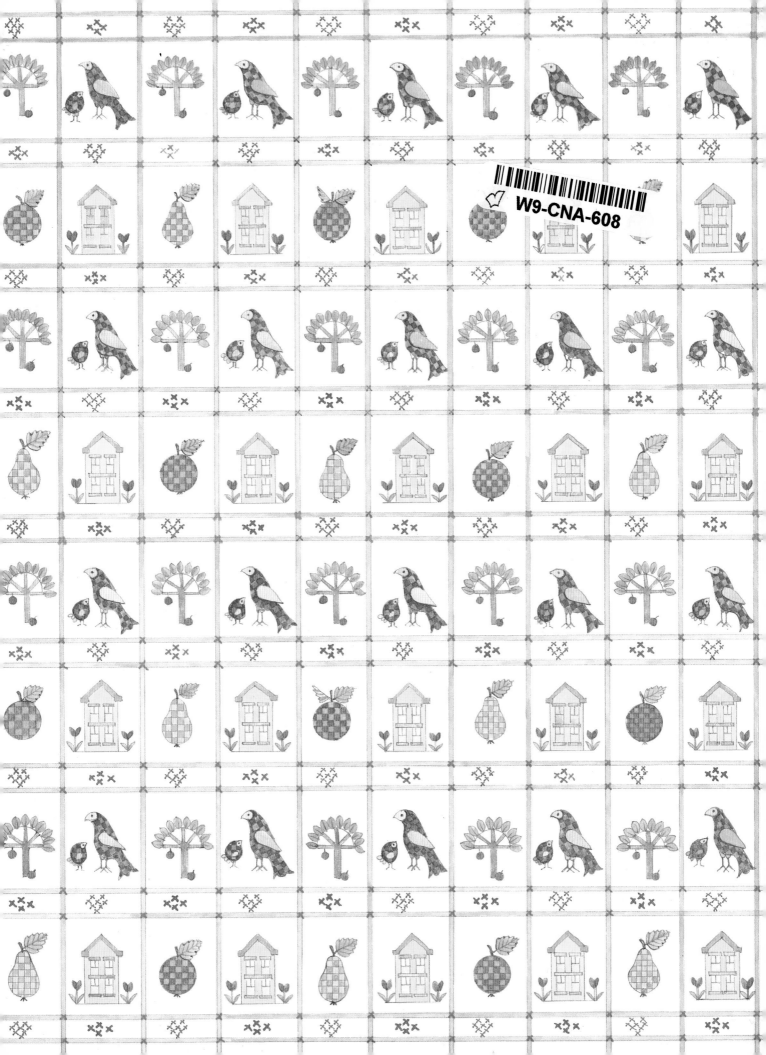

Mom Remembers

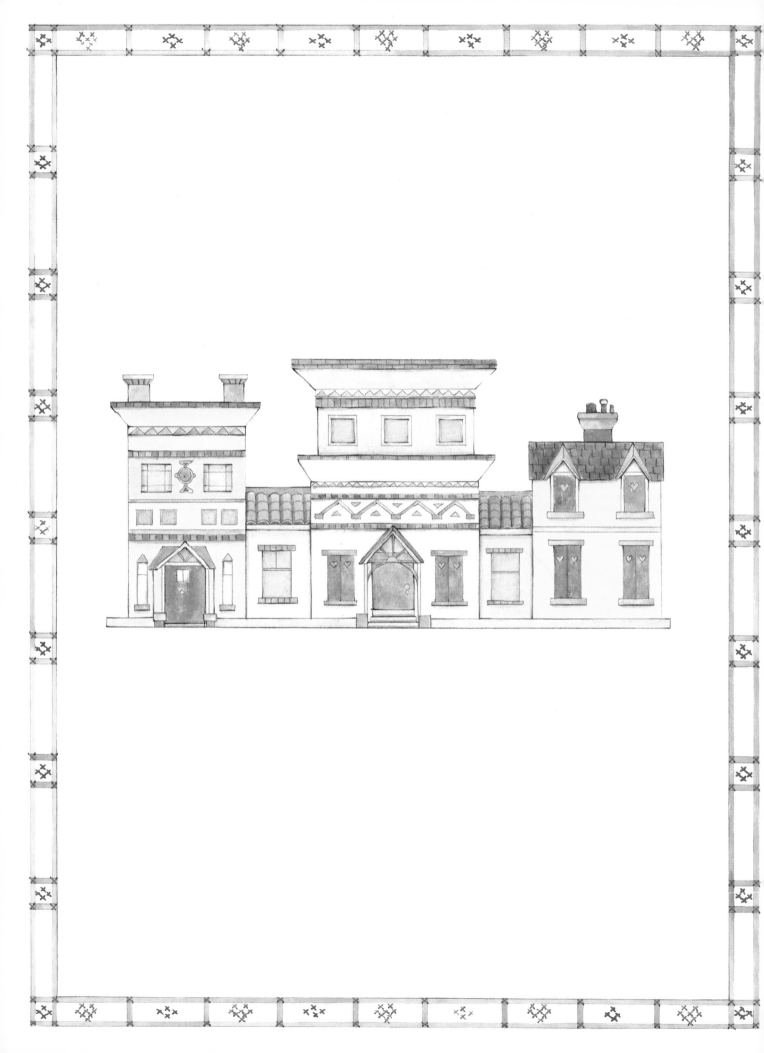

Mom Remembers

A Treasury of Memories for My Child

CONCEIVED AND WRITTEN BY JUDITH LEVY

DESIGNED AND ILLUSTRATED BY JUDY PELIKAN

A Welcome Book

1817

Harper & Row, Publishers, New York

Grand Rapids, Philadelphia, St. Louis, San Francisco,
London, Singapore, Sydney, Tokyo

Edited By Timothy Gray
Text copyright © 1990 by Judith Levy
Illustrations copyright © 1990 by Pelikan Inc.
Printed and bound in Singapore

For information, address:
Harper & Row, Publishers
10 East 53rd Street
New York, New York 10022
ISBN: 0-06-016238-4

The tiny bits of yesterday
Treasured in this book
Will show how much you mean to us
Each time you take a look.

With love for _____

From _____

Date _____

Contents

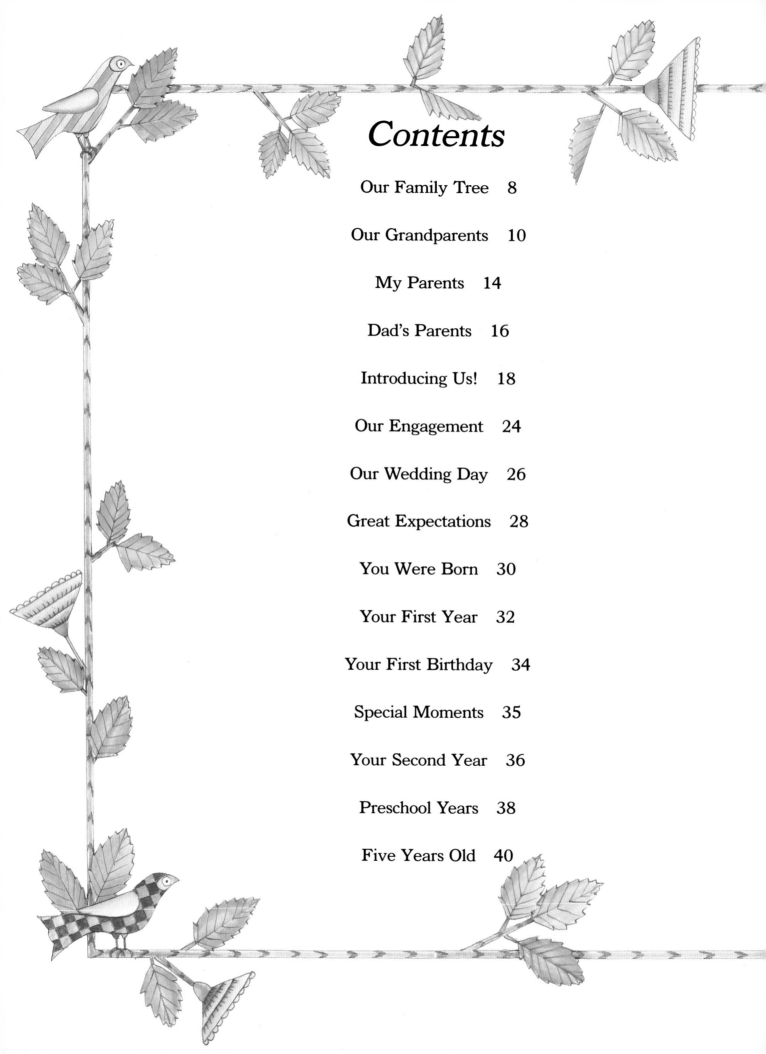

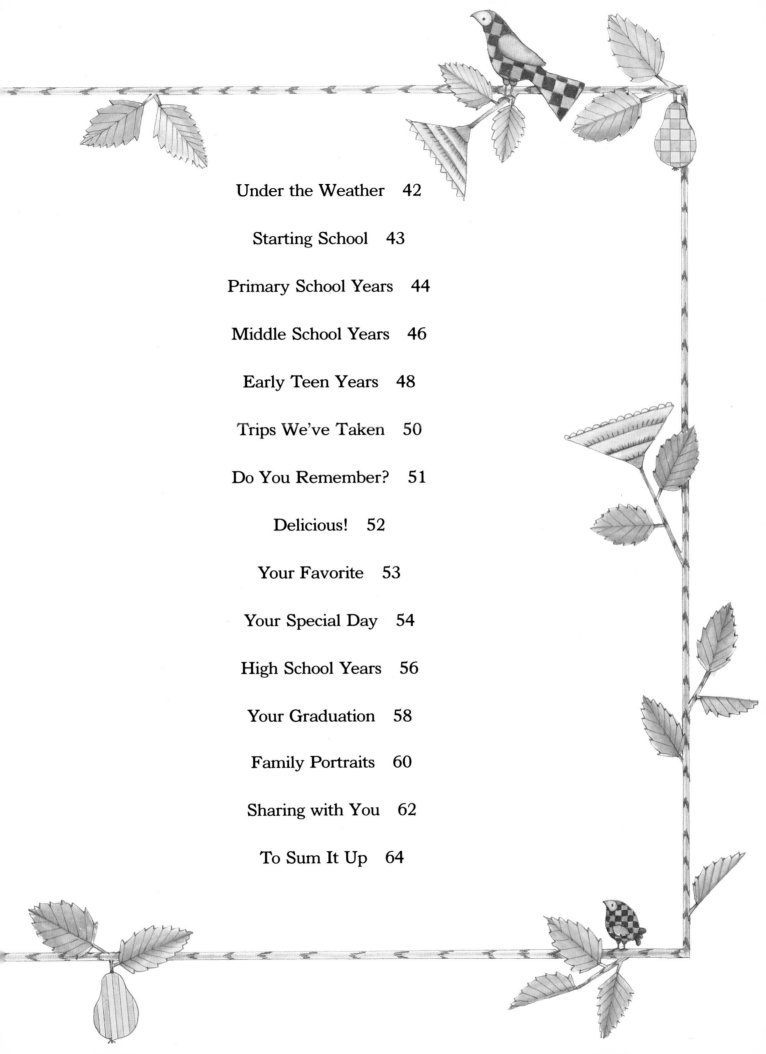

Our Family Tree

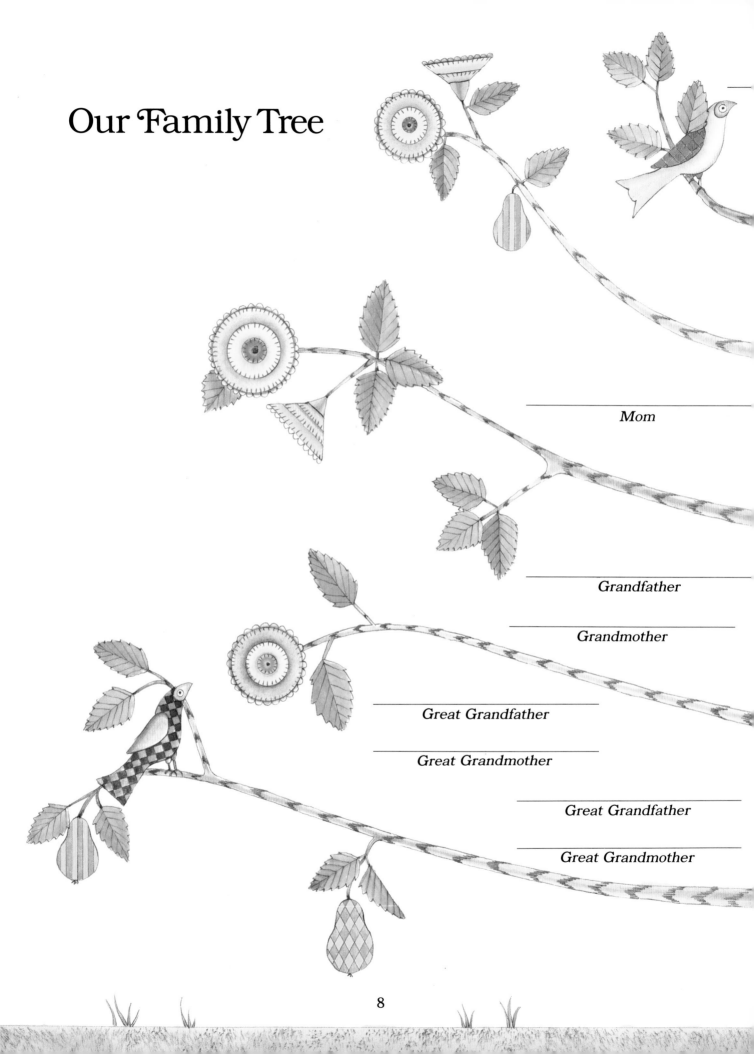

Mom

Grandfather

Grandmother

Great Grandfather

Great Grandmother

Great Grandfather

Great Grandmother

8

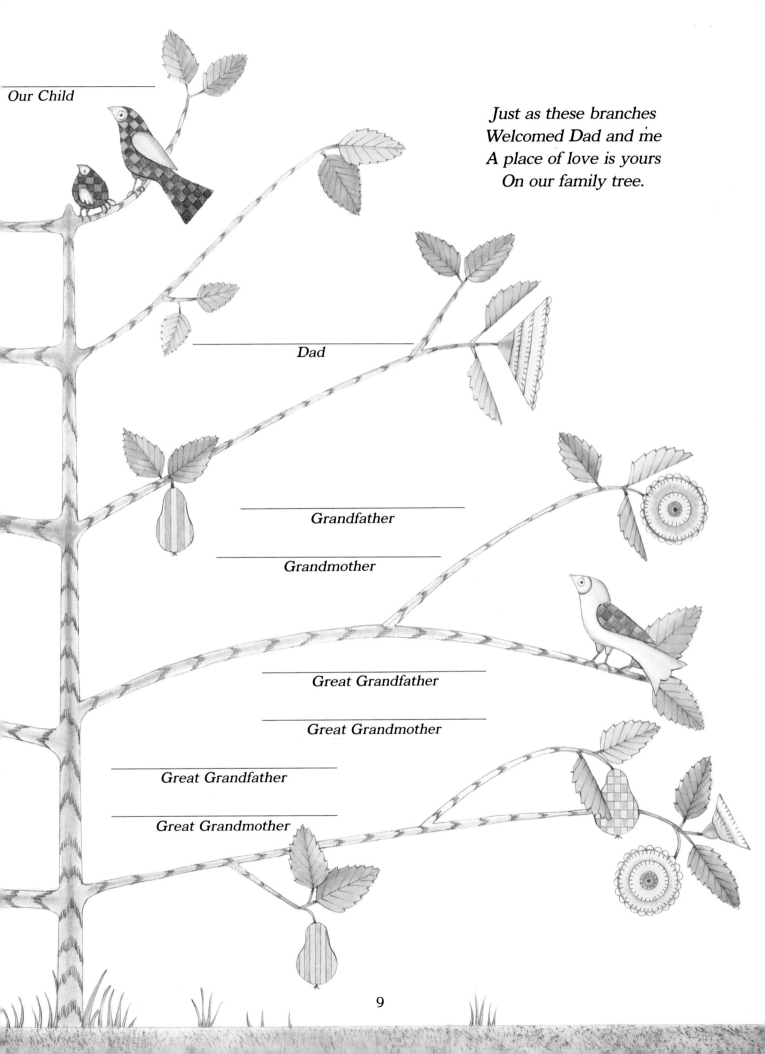

Our Child

*Just as these branches
Welcomed Dad and me
A place of love is yours
On our family tree.*

Dad

Grandfather

Grandmother

Great Grandfather

Great Grandmother

Great Grandfather

Great Grandmother

[PHOTOS OF
MATERNAL AND PATERNAL
GRANDPARENTS]

Our Grandparents

Our Grandparents were a joy
And dear to Dad and me
We think about them often
So very tenderly.

MY MOTHER'S PARENTS

My Grandfather's name _____

My Grandmother's name _____

Their heritage was _____

They made their home in _____

My Grandfather earned his living _____

What I loved most about my Grandfather _____

_____

What I loved most about my Grandmother _____

_____

MY FATHER'S PARENTS

My Grandfather's name _____

My Grandmother's name _____

Their heritage was _____

They made their home in _____

My Grandfather earned his living _____

What I loved most about my Grandfather _____

_____

What I loved most about my Grandmother _____

_____

_____

DAD'S MOTHER'S PARENTS

Dad's Grandfather's name _____

Dad's Grandmother's name _____

Their heritage was _____

They made their home in _____

Dad's Grandfather earned his living _____

What Dad loved most about his Grandfather _____

_____

_____

What Dad loved most about his Grandmother _____

_____

_____

DAD'S FATHER'S PARENTS

Dad's Grandfather's name _____

Dad's Grandmother's name _____

Their heritage was _____

They made their home in _____

Dad's Grandfather earned his living _____

What Dad loved most about his Grandfather _____

_____

_____

What Dad loved most about his Grandmother _____

_____

_____

[PHOTOS OF DAD'S
MATERNAL AND PATERNAL
GRANDPARENTS]

[PHOTO OF MOM'S PARENTS]

My Parents

I was very blessed
Because I always had
Folks that I could count on
The dearest Mom and Dad.

My Father's name _____

My Mother's name _____

They met _____

Their courtship lasted for _____

They were married _____

    DATE: _____

    PLACE: _____

For their honeymoon, they traveled to _____

Their first home was _____

Later they lived _____

My Dad earned his living _____

My folks always praised me when _____

_____

They were very strict about _____

_____

_____

My Mom is special because _____

_____

_____

My Dad is special because _____

_____

_____

Dad's Parents

Dad's folks are wonderful
Dad's folks are smart
Best of all, they loved him
With all of their heart.

Dad's Father's name _____

Dad's Mother's name _____

They met _____

Their courtship lasted for _____

They were married

    DATE: _____

    PLACE: _____

For their honeymoon, they traveled to _____

Their first home was _____

Later they lived _____

Dad's Father earned his living _____

Dad says his folks always praised him when _____

_____

They were very strict about _____

_____

Dad says he will always love his parents because _____

_____

_____

[PHOTO OF DAD'S PARENTS]

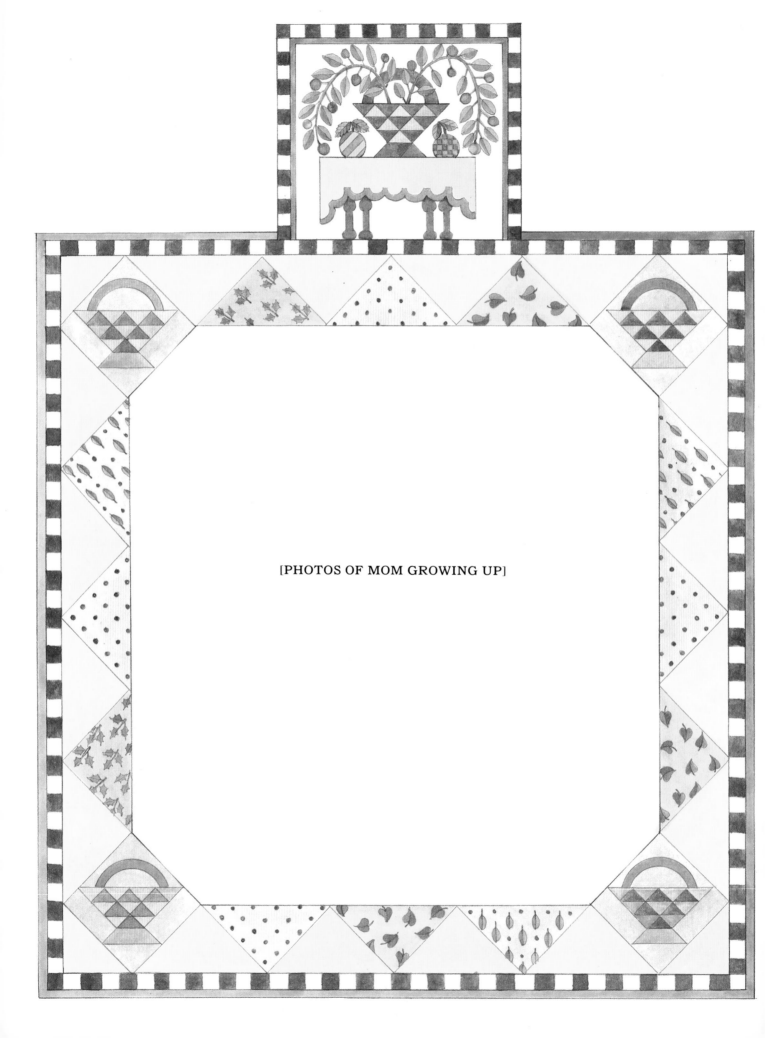

[PHOTOS OF MOM GROWING UP]

Introducing Us!

*Names, dates, and places
And things we used to do,
Happy times and memories
We'd love to share with you.*

I was born on _____

Where _____

I was named _____

That name was chosen because _____

_____

Other members of my family are _____

_____

_____

My best friend was _____

A game I liked to play was _____

A pet I loved was _____

I used to daydream about _____

I always wanted to learn _____

The best trip I ever took was _____

As a teenager I had a crush on _____

I celebrated my Sweet Sixteen by _____

My proudest moment was _____

I was grounded once for _____

Schools I attended _____

_____

_____

My ambition was _____

I started dating when I was _____

Growing up, I worried about _____

_____

After high school, I _____

_____

My first job was _____

_____

I still regret _____

_____

The best advice my parents ever gave me was _____

_____

My happiest childhood memory is _____

_____

_____

[MORE PHOTOS OF MOM GROWING UP]

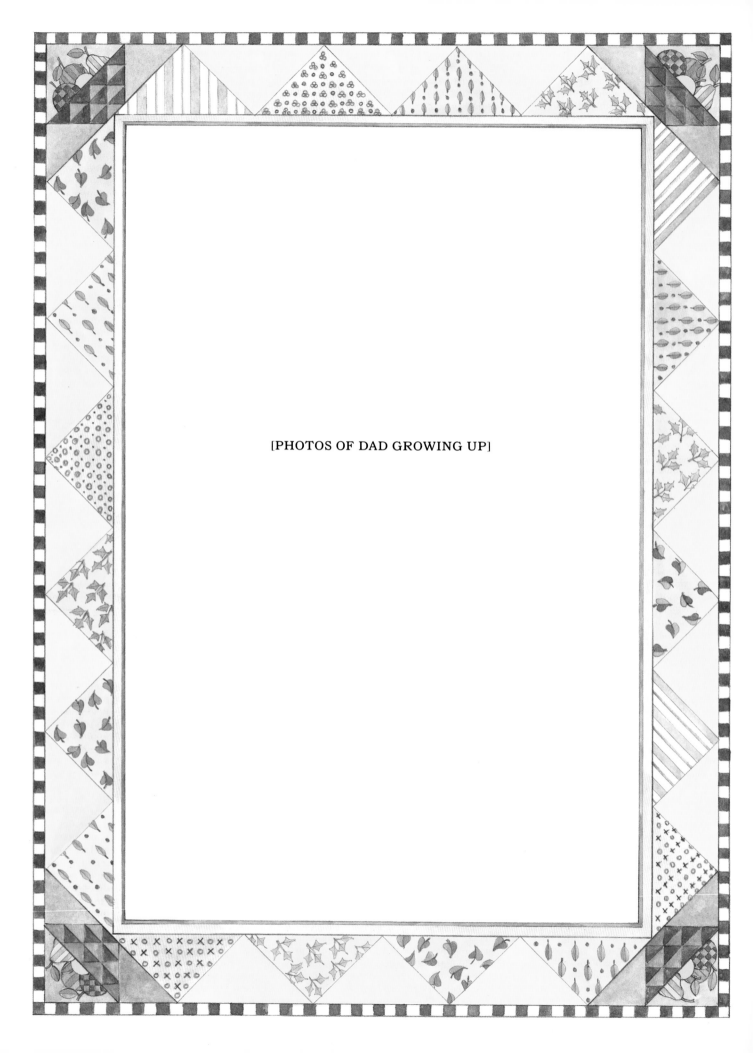

[PHOTOS OF DAD GROWING UP]

Dad was born _____

Where _____

Dad was named _____

That name was chosen because _____

_____

Other members of Dad's family are _____

_____

_____

Schools Dad attended _____

_____

_____

His ambition was _____

Dad began driving at the age of _____

His first car was _____

Dad started dating when he was _____

Growing up, Dad was concerned about _____

_____

After high school, Dad _____

_____

Dad's first job was _____

_____

Dad says his happiest childhood memory is _____

_____

_____

[PHOTO OF THE YOUNG COUPLE]

Our Engagement

*I wanted Prince Charming
I'd have nothing less
When Dad asked to marry me
Of course I said "Yes!"*

Dad and I met _____

I liked him because _____

Dad says he liked me because _____

We dated for _____

When Dad proposed to me, he said _____

We celebrated by _____

The date of our engagement was _____

My parents' reaction was _____

Dad's parents thought _____

_____

Our friends thought _____

_____

I'll always remember this time of my life because _____

_____

_____

[OUR WEDDING PICTURE]

Our Wedding Day

Our hearts beat as one
As we stood together
Husband and wife
For always and ever.

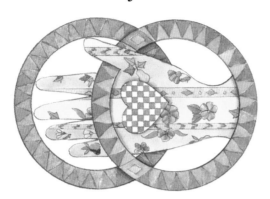

Dad and I were married

DATE: _____

TIME: _____

PLACE: _____

OFFICIATED BY: _____

My wedding dress was _____

On my head, I wore _____

Something old _____

Something new _____

Something borrowed _____

Something blue _____

My Maid of Honor was _____

Dad's Best Man was _____

Dad wore _____

What I remember most about our wedding day is ____

_____

To celebrate our wedding, we _____

For our honeymoon, we _____

27

[PHOTO OF MOM EXPECTING]

Great Expectations

Jumping for joy
We simply went wild
The best news of all—
We were having a child.

I was sure I was going to have a baby when _____

_____

My first reaction was _____

_____

Dad's reaction was _____

_____

When we told your Grandparents, they _____

_____

The doctor who delivered you was _____

The hospital I chose was _____

I gained _____

Names we considered for a girl _____

Names we considered for a boy _____

To prepare for you, we _____

_____

My due date was _____

Some babies kick a lot, and you _____

[PHOTO OF
MOM, DAD, AND BABY
AND BIRTH ANNOUNCEMENT]

You Were Born

They placed you in my arms
And all my dreams came true
Nature, love, and heaven
Were all wrapped up in you.

Your arrival:

WHERE: _____

DATE: _____ TIME: _____

WEIGHT: _____ HEIGHT: _____

HAIR: _____ EYES: _____

We named you _____

That name was chosen because _____

When I first held you, I _____

_____

Dad's reaction was _____

_____

The first people Dad called were _____

For feeding, I _____

_____

I stayed in the hospital for _____

Preparations for you at home were _____

_____

I thought you resembled _____

A newspaper headline that day was _____

[PHOTO AT ONE YEAR OLD]

The First Year

You're delicious and adorable
As parents, we are blessed
Of all the babies in the world
We have the very best.

Your disposition the first year was generally _____

_____

You were fascinated with _____

_____

If you fussed, Dad and I would _____

_____

Once you could move on your own, you always got into _____

_____

Your first foods were _____

_____

Your favorite was _____

But you refused to eat _____

Your favorite toy was _____

It got so old that _____

A game I played with you was _____

You loved it when Dad _____

The first holiday we spent together was _____

Your First Birthday

You're so very precious
As anyone can see
Special, warm, and wonderful
So dear to Dad and me.

We celebrated your first birthday by _____

_____

People who shared that special day were _____

_____

Gifts you received were _____

_____

For your birthday, we served _____

_____

You were cutest when _____

_____

A newspaper headline that day was _____

Your first year certainly was _____

_____

As you started your second year, Dad and I hoped _____

_____

_____

Special Moments

So many firsts
We want to recall
The sunshine and smiles
Let's remember them all.

Your first tooth appeared at _____

You started crawling at _____

You started to walk at _____

Your first word was _____

Your first haircut was _____

The first time you smiled at me, I _____

_____

The first time I fed you, I _____

A song I used to sing to you was _____

The first time you slept through the night, I _____

You were so cute when _____

_____

We always remember the time you _____

_____

We're glad you're our baby because _____

_____

[PHOTO AT TWO YEARS OLD]

Your Second Year

What a big little person
You turned out to be
Two years old and precious
To Daddy and me.

In your second year, you were cutest when _____

_____

You always mispronounced _____

You would say _____

If I held the telephone to your ear, you would _____

_____

Your favorite song was _____

Your favorite nursery rhyme was _____

Your favorite treat was _____

When you woke up in the morning, you would _____

_____

As far as thumb-sucking went, you _____

_____

Your average night's sleep was _____

In the crib, you had to have _____

_____

By now you could say _____

[PRESCHOOL PHOTO]

Preschool Years (Ages 3-4)

You're fun, you're warm and caring
You're nice as you can be
You bring joy and happiness
To your Dad and me.

During the week, you _____

On weekends, we _____

_____

By now, you were grown up enough to _____

_____

When you played with other children, you _____

_____

When it came to sharing your toys, you _____

_____

Visits to the doctor were _____

_____

Bedtime was a time when _____

_____

Dad and I loved most when you would _____

_____

As a child, you were _____

_____

When it came to giving hugs and kisses, you _____

_____

[PHOTO OF FIVE YEARS OLD]

Five Years Old

Being five is special
Being five is fun
Candles, love, and birthday cake
And hugs from everyone.

This year was special because _____

_____

You lost your first tooth _____

Your bedtime was _____

You loved to be read _____

You enjoyed playing with _____

You're so grown up at five, because _____

_____

We celebrated your birthday by _____

_____

_____

People who celebrated with us were _____

A birthday wish for you _____

_____

We're so proud of you because _____

_____

Here's the way you print your name _____

Under the Weather

It would break our hearts
More than words could tell
'Cause you were so unhappy
And just not feeling well.

Childhood illnesses you had were_____

_____

We always knew you weren't feeling well when_____

_____

We worried so the time_____

_____

When it came to taking medicine, you_____

_____

To keep you occupied, we_____

_____

Your doctor's name was_____

When you would see him_____

Your favorite under-the-weather meal was_____

_____

To pamper you, we would_____

_____

We could always tell you were feeling better when_____

_____

Starting School

Your first day at school
Was filled with hope and fear
I smiled till I walked away
And then I shed a tear.

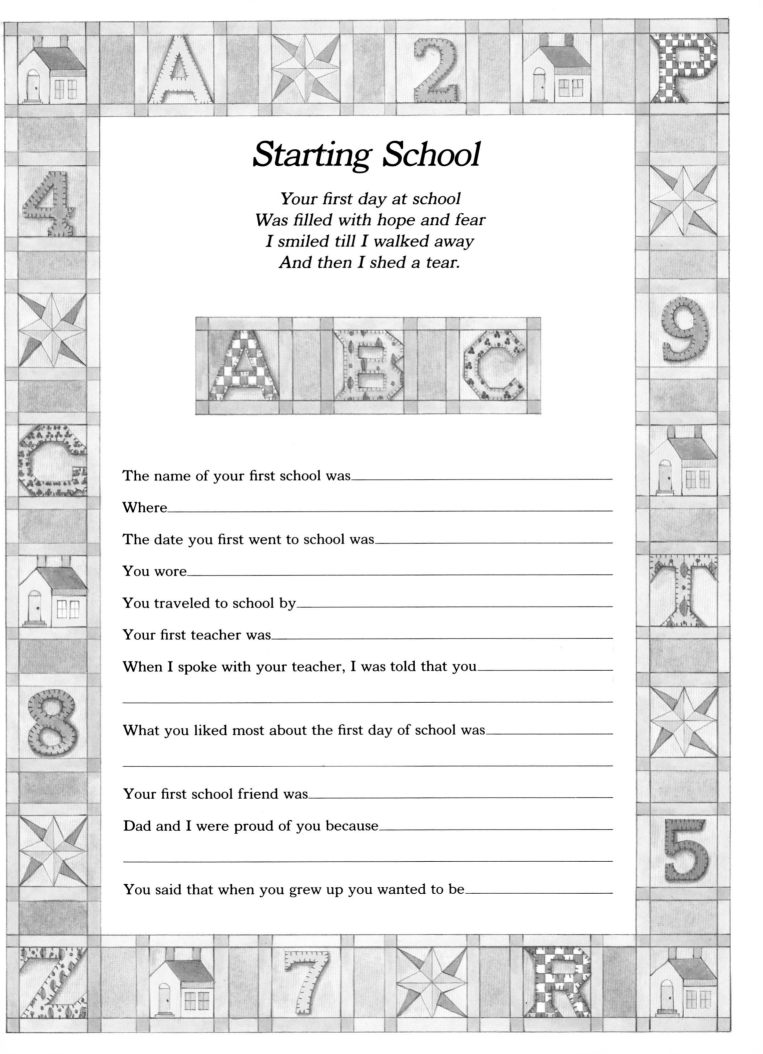

The name of your first school was_____

Where_____

The date you first went to school was_____

You wore_____

You traveled to school by_____

Your first teacher was_____

When I spoke with your teacher, I was told that you_____

_____

What you liked most about the first day of school was_____

_____

Your first school friend was_____

Dad and I were proud of you because_____

_____

You said that when you grew up you wanted to be_____

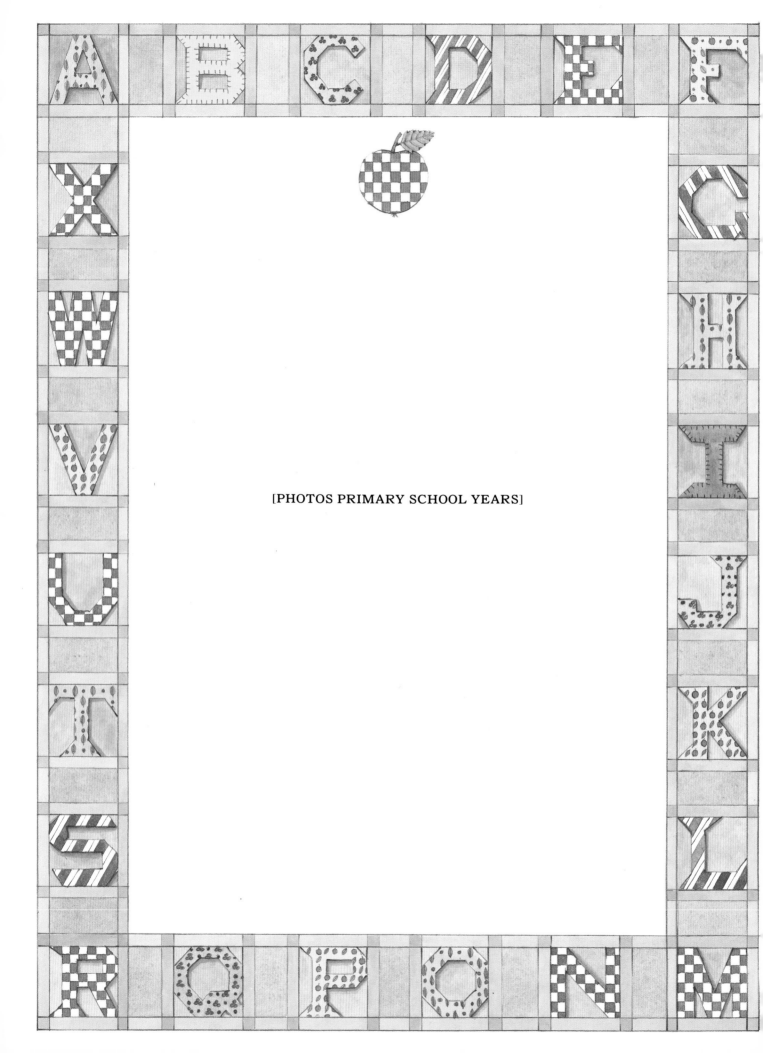

[PHOTOS PRIMARY SCHOOL YEARS]

Primary School Years (Ages 6-8)

Time passes quickly
Still it comes as a surprise
How very much you've grown
We just can't believe our eyes.

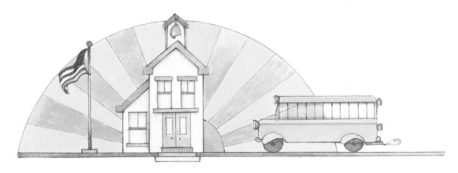

Your favorite primary school subject was _____

Your favorite primary school activity was _____

Your teachers were _____

_____

_____

Your best school friends were _____

_____

You enjoyed spending time after school _____

_____

We'll always remember these years because _____

_____

_____

We were so proud of you because _____

_____

A thought I'd like to share with you _____

_____

_____

Your signature _____

Middle School Years (Ages 9-11)

It's not like us to brag
But we've just got to crow
Because you're really wonderful
And we wanted you to know.

We'll always remember these years because _____

_____

In general, you thought school was _____

Your teachers were _____

_____

_____

On weekends, you loved to _____

_____

During the summers, you _____

_____

You seemed so grown up because _____

_____

Your best friend was _____

Your room was always _____

_____

You once got into hot water because _____

_____

We're so proud of you because _____

_____

Your signature _____

[PHOTOS MIDDLE SCHOOL YEARS]

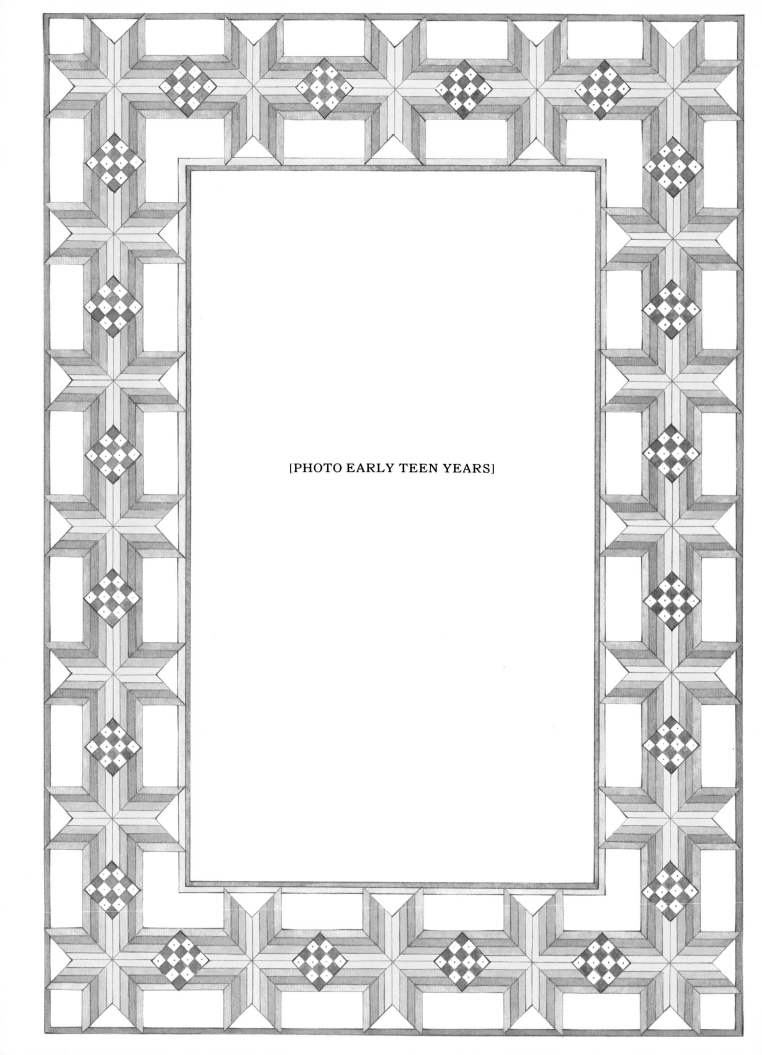

[PHOTO EARLY TEEN YEARS]

Early Teen Years

So many challenges
You've surely passed the test
You always make us very proud
Because you are the best.

We can count on you to _____

_____

When it comes to spending money, you _____

_____

When it comes to saving money, you _____

_____

These years at school were memorable because _____

_____

Your favorite teacher was _____

Your best friend was _____

Your ambition was _____

After school, you _____

_____

Summer vacation was spent _____

_____

We'll always remember these years because _____

_____

_____

_____

49

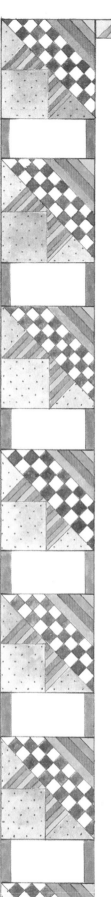

Trips We've Taken

It's really nice to travel
So many things to see
But after all is said and done
Home's where we want to be.

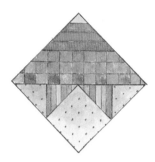

Your first trip was to _____

Your age was _____

We traveled by _____

As a traveler, you _____

To keep you interested on the journey, I _____
_____

You always wanted me to bring along _____
_____

When it came to flying, you _____

You had the most fun when we went to _____

Your most exciting trip was to _____

You loved it because _____
_____

My most vivid memory of a trip we've taken is _____
_____

Other trips you've taken are _____
_____

A place you still want to travel to is _____

Do You Remember!

When our family gets together
There's lots of reminisces
Stories told and told again
With lots of hugs and kisses.

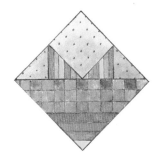

We always laugh about the time _____

_____

You were so cute when _____

_____

One Halloween, you dressed up as _____

Other Halloween costumes were _____

_____

For Mother's Day, you once gave me _____

One Father's Day, you gave Dad _____

We came to see you in school when you _____

_____

One summer, you _____

_____

We still remember when you _____

_____

We were so proud when you _____

_____

_____

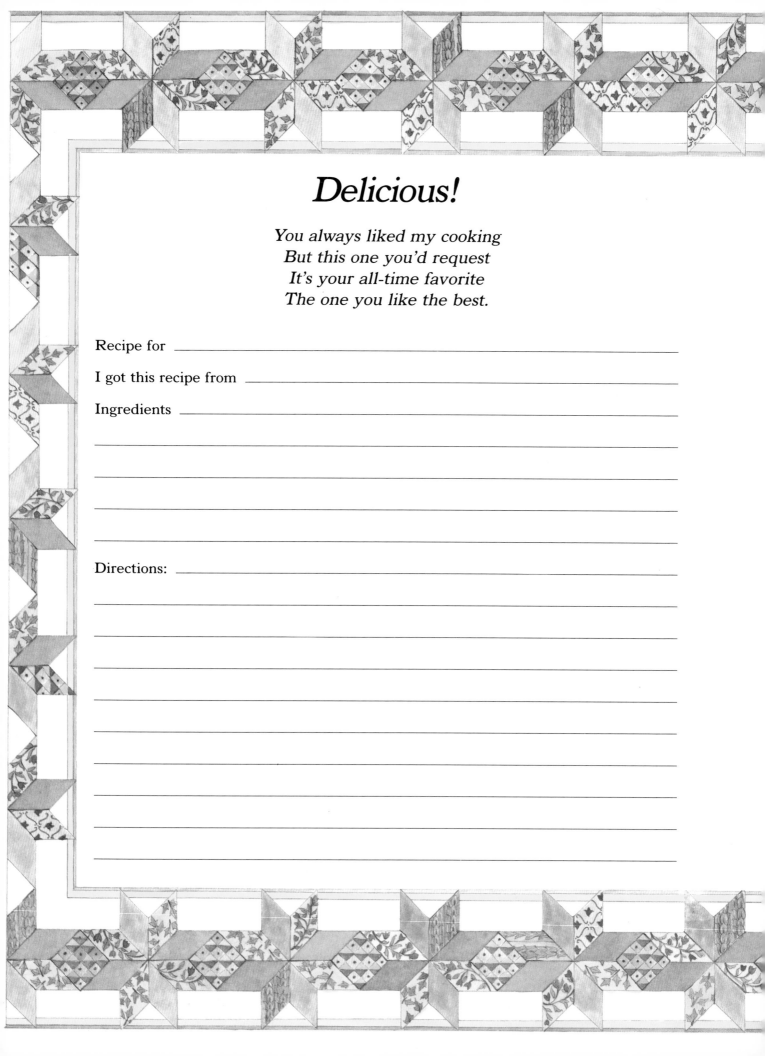

Delicious!

*You always liked my cooking
But this one you'd request
It's your all-time favorite
The one you like the best.*

Recipe for _____

I got this recipe from _____

Ingredients _____

_____

_____

_____

_____

Directions: _____

_____

_____

_____

_____

_____

_____

_____

_____

_____

Your Favorite

I won't say you're choosy
Or anything of the kind
But you're sure about your favorites
Once you've made up your mind.

Song _____

Singer or Singing Group _____

Actor _____

Actress _____

Movie or Television Program _____

Season _____

Holiday _____

Color _____

Flower _____

Participator Sport _____

Spectator Sport _____

Sports Team _____

Food _____

Junk Food _____

Book _____

Magazine _____

Animal or Pet _____

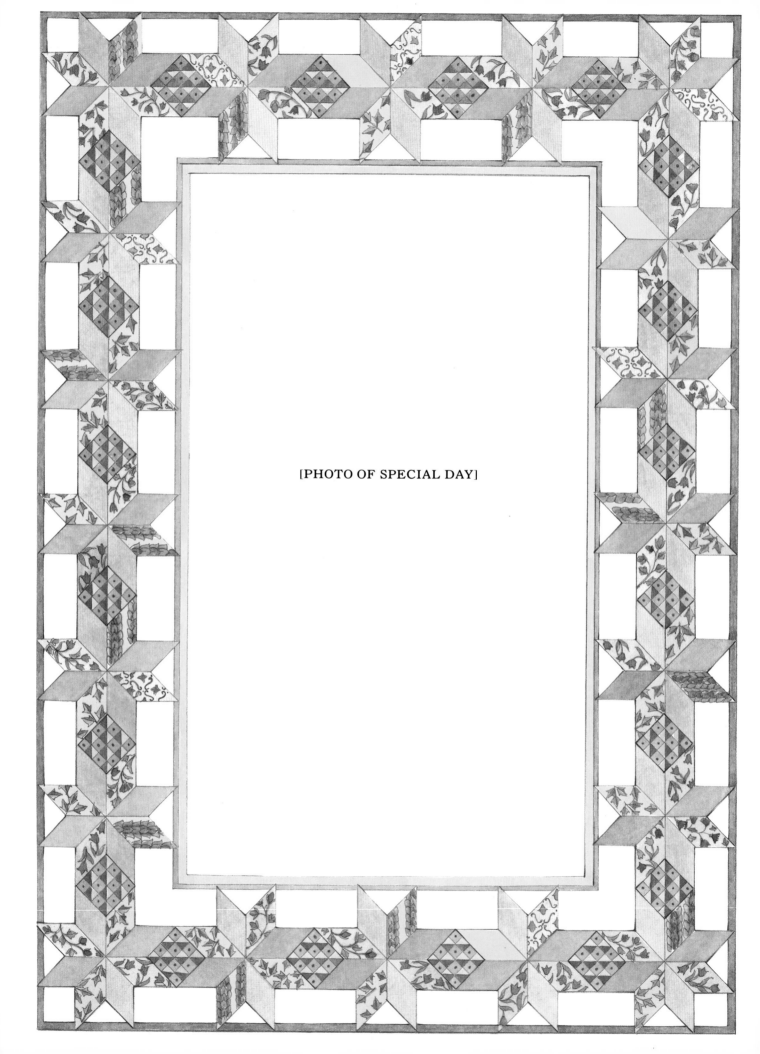

[PHOTO OF SPECIAL DAY]

Your Special Day

Everyone was so excited
A time to celebrate
You made us all so proud of you
And yes, you sure looked great.

A very special day for you was _____

You prepared for this day by _____

_____

You wore _____

It was special because _____

_____

_____

We celebrated by _____

_____

People who joined the celebration were _____

_____

We were so proud of you because _____

_____

We'll always remember this day because _____

_____

_____

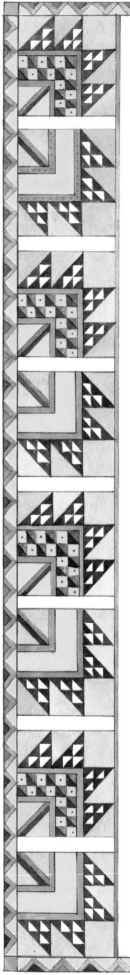

High School Years

When you were just a child
We wanted to inspire you
Now that you're a young adult
How we love and admire you.

The high school you attended was _____

Your best subject was _____

Your grades were generally _____

Your favorite teachers were _____

_____

_____

You usually did your homework _____

_____

A special interest of yours was _____

_____

Your best friend was _____

After school, you _____

_____

_____

You showed talent in _____

_____

_____

_____

Your allowance was _____

You usually spent it on _____

_____

_____

For extra spending money, you _____

Your jobs around the house were _____

_____

On weekends, you _____

_____

_____

In summer, you would _____

_____

Dating began _____

We were very strict about _____

_____

Curfew on weekdays was _____

Curfew on weekends was _____

For transportation, you _____

You were grounded once for _____

_____

You really had a crush on _____

When it came to the telephone, you _____

_____

Your room looked like _____

Your Graduation

Your future is bright
So much expectation
We wish you the best
Happy graduation!

You were graduated from _____

The date you graduated was _____

You celebrated your graduation by _____

_____

After high school, you planned _____

_____

_____

Your ambition was _____

What Dad and I remember most about those high school years _____

_____

_____

_____

_____

We're so proud of you because _____

_____

_____

[GRADUATION PHOTO]

Family Portraits

The greatest fools are people
Who've lost touch with their own
Families are the greatest gift
The world has ever known

This photo was taken on _____ at _____

These special family members are: _____

_____

_____

_____

I love them so much because _____

_____

_____

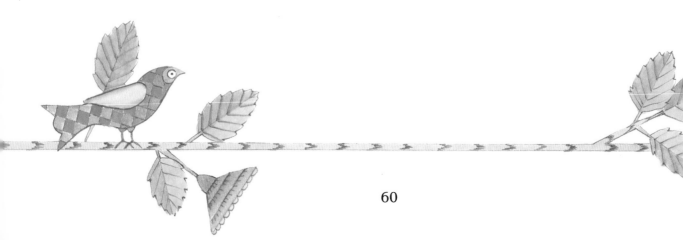

[PHOTO OF MOM'S FAMILY]

This photo was taken on _____ at _____

These special family members are: _____

_____

_____

_____

Dad loves them so much because _____

_____

_____

[PHOTO OF DAD'S FAMILY]

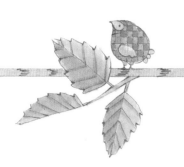

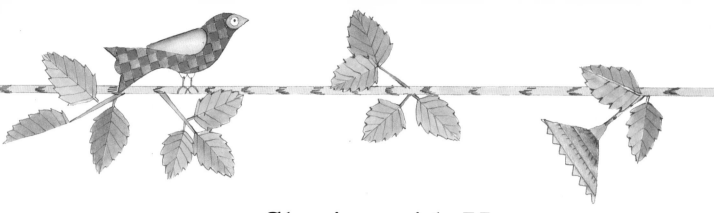

Sharing with You

Our deepest values are _____
_____
_____
_____

We think the key to happiness is _____
_____
_____
_____

We used to feel strongly about _____
_____
_____

Now we feel differently and believe _____
_____
_____

We still like the old-fashioned ways of _____
_____

Sometimes we find it hard
To let anyone see
Just what counts the most
To your Dad and me.

But we prefer the modern ways of _____

_____

_____

We think young people are wiser today about _____

_____

_____

We would always like you to _____

_____

_____

_____

We will always love you so much because _____

_____

_____

_____

_____

_____

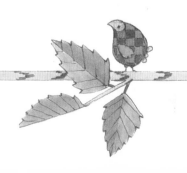

To Sum It Up

You'll always be my baby
Though the years go by
You're my heart of hearts
A lucky mother, I.

[A RECENT PHOTO OF THE FAMILY]

My wish for the future is _____

_____

_____

_____

_____

_____

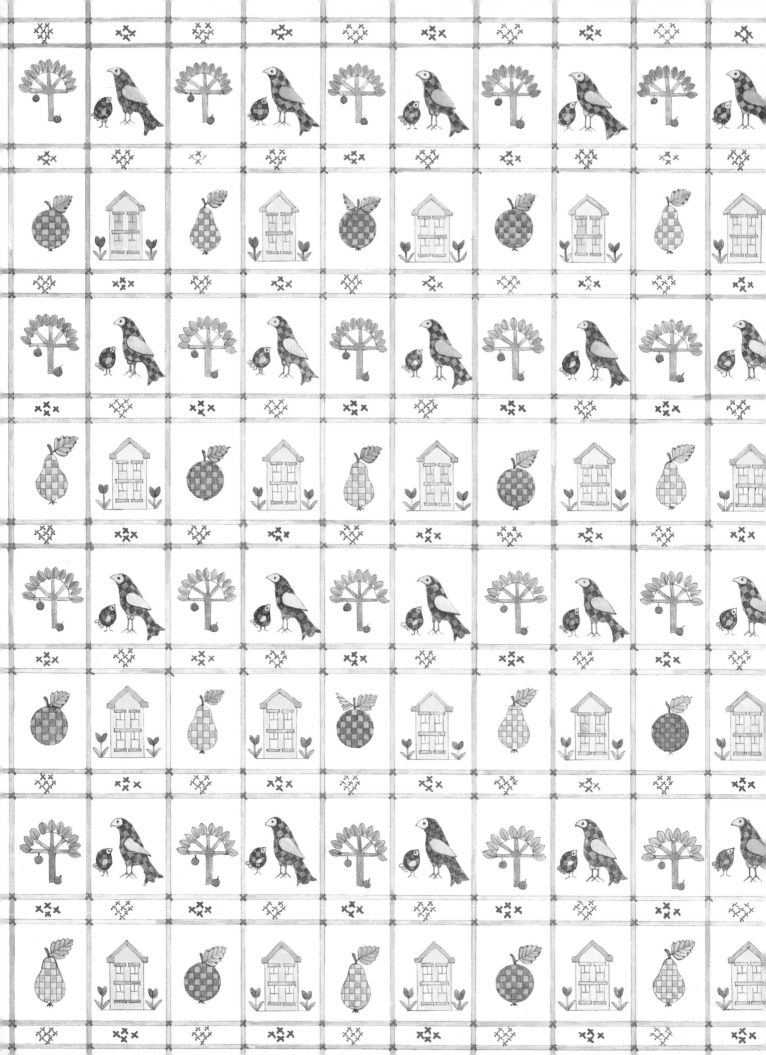